REQUISITES

REQUISITES

Ramya Chamalie Jirasinghe

Requisites
published in the United Kingdom in 2025
by Mica Press & Campanula Books

https://micapress.uk | contact@micapress.uk

ISBN 978-1-869848-42-2

Copyright © Ramya Chamalie Jirasinghe 2025

The right of Ramya Chamalie Jirasinghe to be identified as the author of this work has been asserted by her in accordance with the Copyright, Designs and Patents Act of 1988.

All rights reserved.

for the guardians of our Earth
and
the six seekers journeying upstream

CONTENTS

PREFACE

REQUISITES

OUTER ROBE
unmasking
this good earth
drill baby drill
barefoot
we return to the question

INNER ROBE
some are more vulnerable than others
opening doors
this is the truth we must face

CLOAK FOR WINTER
warp & weft
shelter
this story
stars
carrying logs
we have known fire

BOWL
refills
mango season
someone will take home this harvest
ingredients for a pie
fish kedgeree
the dog at the dining table

THE MIDDLE PATH

ritual
looking into this bowl again

RAZOR
edge of day
pruning
ouroboros
cleaving
this can't be the way to the garden

NEEDLE & THREAD
    strips of cloth
    what can we repair
    unravelled
    weaving the sun

WATER STRAINER
    thirst
    filters
    the shore

BELT
    more on holding it together
    where our journeying brought us
    Indian Rope Trick
    cetanā
    interheartsphere

                ABNEGATION

PREFACE

By Leslie Bell, Mica Press

Ramya Jirasinghe's *Requisites* is a steady iteration of the problem of high living in a world where nature is both disappearing through industrialisation and threatening, as the climate is altered by human agency, to produce unbearable temperatures for humans. In no uncertain terms it prescribes the ancient medicine for our ills, the Way of the Buddha. Shedding possessions, keeping no more than necessary, realising the truths: of suffering, the cause of suffering (craving), the ending of it, and the path to take to end suffering. With her focus on the modern world, she writes 'this is the truth we must face' and 'we looked the self in the eye / and saw a masquerade of light' … 'we must not forget we are on a journey to the heart: / self-destruction is not our intention.' As a publisher, I was immediately captured by the sincerity and scope of these poems from Sri Lanka, their urgency and relevance for a worldwide readership.

REQUISITES

the river flows relentlessly - we are on its banks:
"Step in." "Step in."

now is the time for going upstream, against
the words of the world, iron yokes binding us.
signboards spurned.

5th Century BC: dawn tumbles on treetops, truth streams from a Buddha
snakes coil underfoot, there is and will always be rain, pouring
between seasons of thirst.
he told of his journey -
tracing this river swimming in circles
a hot coal clenched in the fist -
everything is burning.
wade through this river, braving eddies and swirls.

21st Century: what will be offered to the Baby Boomers
Gens X, Y, Z, A who step out?
along the way, there will be others who will join
from cities of the future
leaving the SUV, the double-door fridge,
the pinstriped suit, the holiday in Majorca.
they who will tread upstream
sallied pavements on Friday nights
dressed in linen jackets or spaghetti strap cocktail dresses with six rounds
down, went for vindaloo after the last call
that was us. he wandered a land, searching; you and I will do the same
in city malls railway waiting rooms airport lounges.

what happens if we don't spurn the river. that is not the question.

this is the question: is there a way to appease the sun
our backs stripped of covering, sans SPF60
as we hurtle pell-mell into flames.

that falconer of boundless hearts
travelled light – eight requisites strung on the body

an outer robe
an inner robe
a cloak for winter
a bowl for food
a razor
needle & thread
a water strainer
a belt

could we accept, we who need so much for everything, that

we are the sun we are the burning

we the burnt we the arsonists.

OUTER ROBE

there are ways to recycle our raiment
the South Asian immigrant rustling through bins
in the charity shop bringing into the air
the crumpled weight of days wrung out on a lifeboat
boot loads of frippery, best bib and tucker, prêt-à-porter
loungewear, haberdashery and trim
stuffed into a tea chest shipped to the outer edges of
the world on the back of a
a charity advertising slogan from
servings of large-heartedness
exotica of the gaudy sari a waterfall of fuchsia tumbling
down the sofa in the fashion designer's house

there were other ways to recycle for vestiary: stripping
the funeral shroud before vultures swooped in
unwrapping stained rags restitching them into a life
chosen when the map had no other place to take the wanderer.
these could be vestments for the journey upstream.
these were.

these are not options for us. this is another millennium.

us who wore brocade jackets vicuña dresses wonder
what will be enough for a day and a night a year and a life.
this disentangling of thread that has been woven into the hair
the fine bones of the foot, of these scads of clothes
what is to be denuded.
the shunning must begin

unmasking

this eschewing cannot begin without knowing
what this good earth is spinning towards:
a plastic cola bottle hurtling to the sun
that is how it is for us

how does this good earth look
where it all begins
some do not know
you really do not know

let us show you our good earth unmasked

this good earth

the stream wears the paddyfields
hung long and low along its braids
glistening in grain, moonlight reflecting
off husk on seed waiting
for morning

someone will carry home this harvest
soft rice steaming ladled through a child's bedtime stories
someone praying: "may this child grow strong"
"may this child hold a future glowing and certain."

the harvest sways and shimmers
a fishing cat pads along the bank angling
a nightjar flutters calls in warning

the quiet sound of a child growing fills the village air

from the edge of the field
in this valley of sleeping children
night soil of a fast-fashion workroom
drains into lulling waters at high waist. swirling indigo
turns fish into mountain climbers worn out for air
washes the stone bed
to the Barn Owl's call
acid washed stone
raw washed stone
enzyme washed stone
bleach washed stone
vintage washed stone

this is our good earth

In next year's national budget, there may be a small allocation for a dialysis centre close to the villages in the north central provinces if the remittances improve and the deficit narrows.

someone will carry home this harvest

the cat slides into the river
cobalt fish weave through its claws
the nightjar calls: rivet—ed/ rivet—ed/ rivet—ed/

drill baby drill

Mad Dog
truss spars a snarl
of veins into the gulf

fracking rocks

the seabed trembles
such molestation is no match
for poseidon once shaker of the earth.
this new age of rending shred even the innards of once invincible gods retching
ocean water back to its owners: bluefin tuna
steeped in radium two two six. hauled

on to land from this tank marinated in oil and slick
they sizzle in the pan.
even muskrats gnaw on the same fillets.

                              barefoot
we will
just do it

this beginning of going barefoot, this season of refusal
this slow discarding of those extra extra extra things.

we unfurl the cord that is strung from our neck
tethering us to a thousand dazzling this that other things
desire and seduction the duty-free, the koningsstraat,
eros dancing in the circus, laughing babies in
jars behind the bevelled sweetshop window

our unknowing led us deeper and deeper into the river
pulsating to this gull that was sung in our ears:
"in the buying there is everything and all"
those were the emperor's new clothes
only a few shouted out:

"but these cover nothing"

we listened. you and i.

                    we return to the question

i lied.
the lie was this: we listened

when dolphins streamed into canals
in the sinking city wearing plastic morettas
when haze cleared the sky
when peacocks crossed the highway
and strutted into Babel

that masquerade of the twenties
when a novel plague fell upon our homes

we thought we listened
only that, us emperors in new clothes
had not

and so return to the question
us dangling from skyscrapers at high noon
can we appease the sun

INNER ROBE

then there are matters of self and other
of lines and boundaries of othering and queering
of binaries and non - men women enby -
we draw up lingerie walls inner robes

us goldfish in glass bowls blithely puffing bubbles
peering through a convex frame astigmatic

the inner robe a sheath on a body
transforming towards its conclusion
cradling in skeletal arms the self.
alone the heart must brace itself to see
the outer facade etched on skin
crumple to the hospital floor

                some are more vulnerable than others

there was a man who worked in a clinic
he saw so many children, 'twas his endless picnic
he gave them some bon bons, said he was their friend
then unrobed them carefully and took them round the bend

opening doors

there is also respite. gifts on quiet days, given without reason
everything we thought we didn't deserve.
we keep our ear to the smooth shell of loneliness
and listen to waves washing to shore, listening harder
hear a voice beckoning - a calling word we fear to name
we leave in disbelief and return thinking they would have left
gathered by the next wave riding the surging current of better things
but we find them waiting as the soft breathing of
one person who whispers
no one finds the door alone
i will come with you

so there are many going on this journey

you me them us

                    this is the truth we must face

even the inner robe has to be discarded
stripping to the core to that soft pulse in
the heart's centre
calls for the most difficult task:
looking oneself, where?
in the eye.
we are not making fun here

the eye will understand what it sees
only after it is has seen itself

we may permit ourselves the inner robe
after we have dissected the eye
held it to the sun and watched its rays
stream in

we must accept that it was all only light
converging

the shape of the beloved
the dazzling world around us

CLOAK FOR WINTER

so cold so cold so cold
these days and nights and years
after
we looked the self in the eye
and saw a masquerade of light

most of us will now walk upstream
leaving the shopping mall and the
tyre factory ratings that were
oh so so so iron bibs hung round our necks
we realize they wanted us to drive
further and further and further
swept with the tide into
the red streak of raspberry confit
the cucumber foam on the slithering oyster
we now see the catch

we were the lobster dropped
into the pot

after the eye saw itself
such a shivering began at the core
there must be a blanket soft as down
without it we will be heartless

icicles and frozen water cannot face the sun
we must not forget we are on a journey to the heart:
self-destruction is not our intention

warp & weft

to weave a cloak for winter we search
cotton fields back home and find rot:
such was possible
one human to another

we who have seen the dissected eye
the world for what it is
sit down shaking

with heavy heart
slowly draw the warp from the loom
pull the thread tight into kindness
here is the weft
it will hold this blanket together
to warm us in this cold place

this is a necessity: a blanket for
this winter

sit sit stay at this loom
you and i have to learn to weave
we cannot begin until we have
this cloak wrapped
round our hearts

shelter

carrying our winter cloaks so we wander

the outer robes our shields and waving banners
markings we cannot eschew
the colour of our skin, the intonation of the syllable
the place our fathers began to walk from
helping us to look back from where we now stand

all round is the world in a shop window
sold to us through slogans

let us move forward now
so much to carry even after all this discarding

there is still food to think about
a place to lay our head for the night

this story

we come to a clearing as vast as the story we are trying to tell

the ground is shorn of grass the sky of clouds
there were times we believed in our own divinity
with power no one bestowed on us
to make and break the world at whim

to cull the living to unmake the dead
to give breath to AI and hope the world would
remain shielding itself from our onslaughts
to replenish us over and over again

this is the story and its end we no longer need to guess

we will scan the open field before us
and know which way to turn
for winter is already upon us
let us unfurl the cloak

stars

overhead the sky pulls out a cinema reel
of timeless length shutter speed lowered
playing heaven's opaque film
that we take to sleep eyes closed
each pulsating orb a cosmos above us
a sheet of stars

we nod – this is the immutable law
there is only birth and transfiguration
over and over again a recreating
we drink the sustenance of heavens
in this evermoving film
as we swirl through a milky stream
tied to a dream

carrying logs

even the cloak no longer warms us, we have forsaken
our rites: birth and life propelled onwards
the long green shoots that unfurl from the soft earth
in spring, urging snowdrops towards the sun

all round us mornings break in darkness the way
they ended, bringing the flapping of batwings out
as the sun slipped
the dew turned to frost and frost heralded snow
but the sun lashed us with drought

we leave the shelter we have etched out of brick hovels
so different to the glittering cities we left behind
this is no way to begin a day
we know better than to ask for more

this winter cloak a shroud for cover fails, the heart
must guide us out of forsaken landscapes
we understand this - we need fire but know not where
to look the basins have run dry
their names Ghawar Burgan Cantarell Kashagan
Newfoundland read like new
world nursery rhymes in our heads

we gather a handful of leaves on the kitchen floor
lift the wood axe to cleave flotsam
we can no longer wring warmth
from the world around us

we have known fire

still we do not curse this shivering oh we will never
for we have known fire

there was a time we ran gas masked
from front door to next shelter
as the sky poured confetti of ash
we have lived inside fires

all around us there was scorching
we left that, us the fortunate

we think not about those who could not
because we believe we did all we could:
our monthly contribution to the charity

sometimes there is also a burning
when the heart regrets
but the shivering overpowers it all

we do not curse this shivering oh we will never
for we have once been kindle stood in the flare

BOWL

its smooth walls cradled in our palms
a bowl may hold just enough
of all that we need to stand

this body through seasons of
waterless days, silos empty of rice
nights searching for comfort

this feast of abnegation is self-sought
a pleasure that surprises us in savouring
the slow satiation that arises unbidden
from the plenty contained

within this bowl, cradled in our palms,
one apple, an emerald forged by light
a pile of corn, scattered sun slivers,
over them crisp leaf, glistening with dew
in its depths some grain, not far from husk
from its lips the certain pull of cinnamon
such lusciousness held in its spherical depths
so much in one bowl. the clamouring that
lived in our throats bows in silence

refills

those of us on this journey have known the largess of
laissez-faire morphed into new lashings of
goods and servings, a liberal smorgasbord
of appetisers – devilled eggs, prawns on toast, bruschetta.
there was no tiring of things. we refilled
our cups at the fountains of soda pop, watched our
other selves mistake such flowing, over grabbing,
this good life

such was Demeter's bounty, we who were never
out of season scoffed the desolation of Persephone's
partings

plenty and more plenty flew in through our doors
until we could have gagged from it all
yet we keep gorging on salt sweet umami

food is an unlikely place to begin this quest
it may not prompt beginnings of journeys upstream

mango season

the season of mangos came upon us like a swarm of locusts and invited every gaping mouth to store its thick sweet yellow nectar in secret burrows. we thought such places of abundance were elsewhere in the Mediterranean or the alps or on the silk route along the karakoram but sometimes harvests are not about filled baskets. impatient men tossed them from boughs towards waiting children. still green. ripened is the reward for the one willing to stand and wait. for the one who knows hope is a blank cheque that could bounce in the cruellest way. we were not willing to hold the basket long enough until days of ripening. and suddenly all of us waiting at the foot of the trees saw our ghosts rise from the crowns and heard the unspeakable said to us someone will take home this harvest

the children saw more. they confronted us in their middle age
that will be tomorrow, about all our scavenging

we could reply for we knew the answer before
their question. the mango trees had our ghosts hovering
over them looking at us in our sleep like
the oracle of Delphi urging us to know the obvious

to answer was to admit, even knowing we did not do.
so we held the answer to the children's question
like the miser on his deathbed, hanging onto a pair of shoes
that would never walk him down the street again

ingredients for a pie

from the paddock to the counter
deskinned and eviscerated:
of head of cattle 1.3 billion
of head of sheep 1.2 billion
of head of goat 1 billion

the ingredient list weighs in cups:
butter or tallow or lard
eggs - chicken or quail
milk – cow or goat or buffalo
cream - real

we wreathe a puff pastry collar round the pen

it promises to contain the
fattened calf searching for its mother

fish kedgeree

such a long distance travelled
to have snuck on to breakfast tables on winter mornings

this is no cure for a hangover – it sticks in the throat
the smoked haddock de-boned from a colonial trail
sitting next to chicken tikka and butter naan

dogs at the dining table

when buildings collapsed as the army bombarded the city
children clamoured out of their cots and waved
pieces of their arms holding white flags

boys dug under the rubble for their mothers
they found frozen kneading pitta into pillows

relief came after the electricity went out after the water ran dry
after the ambulance stopped on the street mid-way a heart attack

only dogs came scurrying for crumbs from a feast
spread out elsewhere, tables heaving at thanksgiving

THE MIDDLE PATH

some understood the fire sermon, but that is not for novices.
we do not have the modern poet's vision of this wasteland
for us slick oil that floats on waves is our sweet license
we climb up steps to small flats
thinking we will not be undone

this road calls for stilling
a stripping of thought and word and deed
all journeys are for standing in one place

we may hang on to these eight requisites but
the practice is circular we must discard
the requisites before we carry them

beautiful heart listen: the green leaves on mountain slopes
ring out like bells still waters flow reeds bend to
the wafting wind. eternity is the unclenched fist.
nothing held returns the caged lark to the sky
free we turn to each other, kind
harmless, the heart learns rapture

from here we build the world anew

ritual

she is this one and many and all like her who have borne on their back

the weight of love for the flesh she has borne, the flesh that bore her and the flesh that devours her, she will appease, she will redeem she will

satiate. she stirs. we peer in with her. watch with each turn porridge, burgoo, pottage samp, grits, polenta, gruel spoonsful swirl
into the vortex. this will be her

offering to gods who have forsaken her.
this is breakfast for a thousand
suns that will rise with her and seek her
to make sense of the world it has lit

she is he she it they everyone everytime who dine from them
rivers begin here

from their hearts pour soft rain, the quiet moment, the cool recess.
they ladle succour into a bowl and wipe their brow

we breath in relief: theirs a ritual as necessary as the
arrival of spring. we may hope the best for the world

looking into this bowl again

let us return to the humble bowl we started with

wrapped round it a swirling mass of knotted roots

old feuds new fears of days of lack
of exodus and invasion
we watch, us armchair critics, such is our privilege,

a boy on the screen waves a flap of his cheek in our faces
pushes his hand through the pixels. before
we can switch channels, grabs our fattened turkey and flees

this bowl: pewter, iron, steel, copper, clay
is swilling with unmentionables. some of us gag

some are certain now. this journey
upstream is no longer for picking.
when we have had enough
have we
at least you and me

RAZOR

this one
implement is allowed with its multiple uses
its surface reflecting the lover's smooth cheek
the cut bracelets on a girl's wrist

for want of an incision an implement
was found -- shell, shark teeth, stone edge

primordial needs
tumble out of an amygdalian pocket

we must learn to flip steel
and wave it in the face of fear

edge of day

the razor is a requisite given. allowed us. for the inner
the outer. we can slash, must slash from the
root the wild tangle that pulls us into the river

the heart cowers holding back weary so weary of
all it has learnt running through alleys
of such bleak cities

this is for laceration, this
one requisite

pruning

this is what grew on the floor of the alleyways
cactus shoots poison ivy curling up lamp posts
thinking this was all the heart could hold
thinking these were why we are here

we drank in the alleyway darkened by a thicket
then we took the knife and slashed in a mad frenzy
and light streamed in

ouroboros

because we did not end this overfilling of plates or those
penthouses that dangled millionaires suspended in midair
as shanty towns sprawled at our doors, we found
ourselves scrambling into fountains, trying to wave the
burning forest away with flaps of carboard

it did not work, we know. we who fled to
our country homes looking for cool springs.
it could not work we realised: the tail meets
the head, sooner or later

                              cleaving

we peel back the weathered crust on the mountain pass
descending terrace by terrace towards the core
these, our new amphitheatres, vast sparkling
stretches of steps glistening in sunlight
soft fumes rising, fused rust copper grey-silver, into
the scape. here lies the future of our greener world
here, everything we hold and discard, these earths
are not rare. only us willing to use the old over and over
again are so few and far between

             this can't be the way to the garden

so much glass, so many cutting edges, we slashed
this earth of its golden spirals with our knives

out out: wounds cannot heal in this glare of florescent light

in some, primordial memories of the wilderness
of budding vines of fragrant blossoms
of leaf and tree sheltering the heart, remained.
that is also us. that is why we have come so far
together

NEEDLE & THREAD

in quiet rooms small cruelties are stabbed in fine point
long and short stitches create seams and patterns

this is work
embroidered by others
tattooed on the body

on this journey we must unpick them all
the breath quivers and we whisper
stay here stay here
we have come to the end of running from ourselves

strips of cloths

those garments we have been trudging with all this way:
the outer robe, the inner robe, the cloak for winter

are now faded and frayed with wear, no longer
a tight sheath, that clean facade

brushed down by scrub soil
entangled in wild branch, pulling at barbed wire
on the fence

they split, giving in to our body's weight
the tear a gaping doorway: the world enters

calling at the skin, the cloth had secured this bodyland,
from all that is lurking outside, from

them and from them and from them

we pick up thread and needle: the straight tear the three
corned tear the hedge tear slowly carefully
running and whip stitching

under the fading light at the end of day
we darn them back for the body

we have not gone far enough to
know what we need to know

there is more to travel
we still need these cloths

what can we repair

our stiches reknot the weave, ever so fine
thread meanders through the frays.
we must be painstaking when
closing wounds: accumulations of use that have
quietly over and over again
worn fine threads gossamer thin until they snapped

the darn holds; good repair deceives the eye
the hedge tear no longer gapes

we begin again hoping the rest will hold
until we make it
to the end

unravelled

at times we remember: below this skein of thread
there is a pulsing centre of such indescribable beauty

in quiet places, when we hear our own breathing we listen
on still nights when the air softens its ravages the leaves hang
stayed from boughs - emerald weights dangling in the air

the centre speaks light-words of its non-language
arms and fingers claimed, muscle fused into air

a knowing spreads and in a moment of perfect understanding
we pull the thread at its weakest and watch it unloop

stitch by stich by stich and cry as relief spreads
from cell to blood to
bone to muscle to hair to nail to skin

the self crafted, unmade, leaving only light

weaving the sun

this won't do: a middle path cannot be
an eschewing of the land it goes through.
that is not the answer we should have sought
when we began this journey to appease the sun.
let us make this a path to weave the sun back into our grip
now loosened of its ravenous grabbing. we left our demand for
everything on the lower bank, for this new harvesting of the sun
– an ancient prayer on our lips – this is enough for now
taking less and less may we allow every breathing creature home
to its refuge, forest to its bursting bloom, wind to carry only
its song. the path clears its way: come with a heart that listens
to wanting, reply strong and certain "this is all I need".

WATER STRAINER

90% space
we spread this net on water
to sieve the coarse – driftwood, twig, rising thought
swirling eddies from lost loves, crushed spirits

let them strain away

and waiting sitting watching as
everything distils to this:
just breath rising and falling
a body breathing

here the world is held

we have snared the monkey

thirst

let's remember the beginning of this journey

we walked out of cities tongues flicking the air
left a lifetime spent forever looking into showroom
windows sniffer dogs at the perfume counter
drugged on dreams invented in back rooms
of advertising agencies
programmed for yearning

then we woke up gripping the edge of a bed
tired of this thirsting

filters

we were the fish the hare the flying falcon
lashing about tangled in fine netting

the leaving and the journey were only for this
an admission: thirsting we starved ourselves

but we almost drowned, stone strung on net,
dragged to the bottom of the river
as we stumbled at the brink

the shore

almost, but not. the rising flood touched us
and we stepped back from the shoreline

the tide will rise and recede
the shore will bank shell carcass pebble

we moved away and halted
spending the world. all of us.

others joined for they too saw
emerging ahead of us
the interheartsphere
on high ground safe from flood

in this slow quelling of torrents

BELT

to the city wanderer who began this journey stepping
off business class, discarding android lifestyles,
shunning waxed faux leather
this appears of least use: the belt.
a thin or may be thick, strip of length, possibly buckle free

a bag was never mentioned among the requisites
even that which holds all within is not a necessity

then why this. we who haven't hitched a horse
led the cattle home at the lowing
or drawn water from a well

the length of rope the plaited cord
the twisted coir holds no worth until
at the close of the day after miles of trudging we arrive at the end
of our tether and search round us for that which holds
the body and spirit together

not all requisites are material
symbols are essentials too

especially on journeys like these

more on holding it together

we have come this far. eschewed the temptation of the blade
promising eternity sought under bloodied bathwater

temptations are not always of the flesh
it is of giving up of it, that secret wish, the ace we hold,
the trump card tossed at those left behind to clear the table

we looked into the still bath holding steel and turned away
on the floor a cord of light slithered, drawing us out out out
from deep water onto plain

from here we will begin the last lap

             where our journeying has brought us

the world is held in the body

all and everything

the seen
the heard
the tasted
the felt
the smelt
the thought

this is where all this journeying is leading to

Indian Rope Trick

sitting we need no leaning: wall or pillar or post
for bone strung on wire holds upright

we are the rope rising into thin air
we the climber
at the end
guaranteed to
disappear

defibrillators fail to coax
the soft breath to rise
the cord to hold when snapped

finally, we know breath is everything

cetanā

here is an aspiration
that underlies every step
on the path we are on:
may we tell the heart, drawing in a breath,
stay. stay. this wild gnawing of wanting
stay. stay. the opaque sheen that rises
from self-absorption, winding
the heart ever tighter into itself.

this stilling is an intention as good as
the gifts the earth offers us
clear as spring water

            interheartsphere

such hearts will converge, we are confident,
all in one place. remember there was first
you and me and then so many joined us:
they who offered gifts for no reason
refused to leave, their words
called us out of empty rooms.
they too came with us -- such a crowd
more to come -- the lower bank is emptying.

this new gathering of hearts
an ever-widening ring of sharing
and encycling has come to be.
On the high bank a new haven
of beings, of every breathing thing,
living in reverence for themselves the web

together the whole is held. thriving.

ABNEGATION

this is our abnegation: a world pushed back

walking against the current
trees burst with leaf and flower
vines tumbled down emptied skyscrapers

we look at these requisites and find
distillation of choice our lapidary

light refracts through the heart
we know its colour without seeing

our journey upstream was a faceting
of this still point of not wanting

not thing nor word nor metaphor

www.ingramcontent.com/pod-product-compliance
Lightning Source LLC
Chambersburg PA
CBHW042320090526
44584CB00030BA/4132